In the Lake

by Irene Lotito

Editorial Offices: Glenview, Illinois • Parsippany, New Jersey • New York, New York
Sales Offices: Needham, Massachusetts • Duluth, Georgia • Glenview, Illinois
Coppell, Texas • Sacramento, California • Mesa, Arizona

dinosaurs

lake

fish

plants

Dinosaurs live outside the lake.
Fish live inside the lake.

2

Big fish and little fish are in the lake.
Red fish! Yellow fish! Gray fish!
Green plants! All are in the lake.

grass

bug

Dinosaur bends down to eat the grass.
Yellow fish jumps up to eat a bug.

Red fish swims in the lake.
Yellow fish swims in the lake.

Red fish wants to eat.
Yellow fish wants to swim away.

Yellow fish hides.
Red fish waits.
Yellow fish waits.

Red fish goes away.
Yellow fish is safe.